I0653723

FLYING SCOTSMAN

ON TOUR
AUSTRALIA

CHAPMANS
1990

Chapmans Publishers Ltd
141–143 Drury Lane
London W2B 5TB

First published by Chapmans 1990
© in the text Blue Sky Productions Pty Ltd 1990
© in the photographs and illustrations Blue Sky Productions Pty Ltd 1990

ISBN 1 85592 504 4

The right of Blue Sky Productions to be identified as the author of this work
has been asserted by Blue Sky Productions in accordance with the
Copyright, Designs and Patents Act 1988.

Concept and Design
Michael Muter

Written by
John Dudley

Illustrations by
Michael Muter

Photographs by
Leon Oberg
Frank Londy
Heather Coulter
Meredith Kirby
Alan Inglis
Matthew Bowdeen
Michael Muter

Acknowledgements
Our thanks are due to:
Australian Railway Historical Society ACT
Steamrail Victoria
3801 Limited
New South Wales Rail Transport Museum
West Ryde Live Steam Society
State Rail Authority of New South Wales
Australian National Railways
V/Line Victoria

Photoset by Macmillan Production Ltd, London
Manufactured in Hong Kong by Imago

Cover illustration
Flying Scotsman and No. 3801 climbing out of Kyogle, on the border of
New South Wales and Queensland.

Australia
ON TOUR 1988–1989

Autumn 1987 produced a suggestion from the National Railway Museum that, as they were unable to release 'Mallard' for shipment to Australia for the Bicentennial Celebrations twelve months hence, perhaps they could suggest that we were interested in sending No. 4472 Flying Scotsman? What followed can only be described as one of the most exciting, momentous and fulfilling periods in Flying Scotsman's already legendary life.

Walter Stuchbery and his Aus Steam '88 colleagues burned the midnight oil in discussion, raised finance and finally agreed the package for the visit with our people in England. We, in turn, dropped everything to ensure that 'FS' was ready: re-tyring the coupled wheels, fitting air brake equipment to run in Australia, repainting the locomotive and finally undertaking test runs on British Rail to ensure that everything was in working order before leaving our shores in September 1988. What was to turn out to be not just a visit but an extended tour lasted some fifteen months until 4472 arrived back in the Port of London at Tilbury in December 1989.

The achievements made and the records set during 'Scotsman's' year 'down under' are chronicled in this book. We believe that 4472 could be said to have taken Australia 'by storm' and our lasting memories will be of the welcome, co-operation and goodwill that we received from the Australian nation. They turned out in their thousands. The support given to our own small English crew attending the locomotive was equally 100 per cent, both volunteers and full-timers helping to maintain our programme – all 28,000 miles of it!

Looking back in future years we will remember the efforts of so many people to ensure the success of 4472's visit to Australia, but it would be wrong not to mention the kingpins. One is Australian: Wal – Walter Stuchbery; and the other is English: our resident engineer, Roland Kennington. They headed up an operation that will be remembered well into the next century when steam is but a memory with no ashes left.

Would we go again? Without doubt! Thank you Australia and your marvellous people for everything.

The Hon. Sir William McAlpine Bt.,
Henley on Thames,
England

April 1990

Sir Nigel Gresley
LOCOMOTIVE DESIGNER

Sir Nigel Gresley, the creator of A1 Pacific 4-6-0 Flying Scotsman, was one of the most outstanding locomotive engineers of all time.

He was born on 19 June 1876, the fifth son of the Reverend Nigel Gresley, the rector of Natherseale in Derbyshire. After only modest academic success, he left Marlborough College for the London and North Western Region's Crewe workshops and a railway career under the autocratic F.W. Webb, the head of the works. In 1898 he transferred to the nearly new works of the Lancashire and Yorkshire Railway at Horwich, just to the northwest of Manchester. Horwich rejoiced in one of Britain's greatest locomotive innovators, J.A.F. Aspinall. Gresley was in good company. Aspinall's students included Sir Henry Fowler, the Chief Mechanical Engineer of the LMB, and R.E.L. Maunsell who was to become the CME of the Southern Railway. And thus by 1925 three of the four British Chief Mechanical Engineers were former Horwich men.

It was altogether a hectic time for an aspiring young engineer. After Horwich, Gresley took an appointment as Outdoor Assistant to the London and Yorkshire Carriage and Wagon Superintendent. Then in 1901 and newly married he moved to Newton Heath near Manchester to be Assistant Works Manager at the carriage and wagon shops. In the following year he was appointed Manager of the works and two years later, in 1904, he was appointed Assistant Superintendent of the entire Carriage and Wagon Department. But that was little more than an interlude. Twelve months later Gresley resigned and moved to the post of Superintendent of the Great Northern Railway Carriage and Wagon Department. He was just twenty-nine. For the next six years he contributed much to the design and improvement of passenger carriages, particularly for the GNR expresses. The capacity, strength and size of the growing freight fleet also received his attention.

H.A. Ivatt, who had been the Locomotive Chief at the GNR's Doncaster works since 1896, retired in 1911. Gresley was appointed Locomotive, Carriage and Wagon Superintendent in the same year, a position he held until the reorganization of the national network under the Railways Act of 1921 – and the position in which he began to design and build a variety of locomotives.

The new London and North Eastern Railway was the second largest of the four groups created by the Act and the Board of the new group offered the position of Chief Mechanical Engineer on a seniority basis to J.G. Robinson of the Great Central Railway. Shortly due to retire, Robinson declined and suggested that the Board need look no further than Superintendent Gresley. And so, in February of 1923, Nigel Gresley became CME of the London and North Eastern Railway only nine months before his famous creation, Pacific No. 4472 Flying Scotsman, rolled out of Doncaster for its trials.

Gresley, of course, went on to design and build bigger and better locomotives. But it is difficult to imagine that he ever took greater pleasure in anything than in the many records set by No. 4472 in what was, by any standards, a highly competitive era.

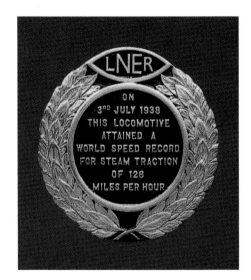

Roland Kennington
CHIEF ENGINEER

A year in Australia, with all expenses paid and time not only to visit every State but to meet thousands of people is an offer no one could decline. And certainly not Roland Kennington. For the Honorary Chief Mechanical Engineer of No. 4472 Flying Scotsman had virtually to live with the locomotive from its arrival in Australia in October 1988 until it was hoisted aboard ship in Sydney for the voyage home 55 weeks later.

The Pacific Class has long been Roland's passion and he was surprised and delighted to be asked to join the Flying Scotsman team in 1985. He swiftly began an almost total rebuild of No. 4472 – the more so when it was announced that Flying Scotsman would be travelling to Australia to take part in the 1988 Bicentennial celebrations.

Roland not only arrived with the locomotive. Throughout that long year he continued to effect both major and minor repairs in extremes of weather to keep Flying Scotsman to its busy operating schedule. He proved the perfect ambassador for both the owners of the locomotive and his country, explaining the mysteries of steam to fans of all ages. With or without No. 4472, Roland Kennington, engineer extraordinary, firmly intends to visit Australia again.

Roland Kennington firing No. 4472.

Opposite: Roland and Reece Muter inspect a 13 cm (5 in) live steam No. 3803 at West Ryde, New South Wales. It was built by Ray Lee of Sydney.

Walter Stuchbery
THE DREAM

It may well have been the model train that he was given for Christmas forty years ago that kindled in Walter Stuchbery the vision of No. 4472 Flying Scotsman arriving in Australia to celebrate the nation's Bicentenary. According to Walter, that gift sparked a passionate interest in matters railway that led him to the Chairmanship of Aus Steam '88, the body charged with the creation of a steam spectacular for the 1988 celebrations.

Walter was born and has spent his life in the tiny rural centre of Yarrambat, some 32 km (20 miles) north of Melbourne. The son of a dairy farmer, Walter put the property into beef cattle ten years ago and since 1970 has doubled up with the Australian Post mail contract for the Yarrambat district. He is the local 'postie' to this day.

Walter has followed his enthusiasm for steam all over the world. He has visited Britain and led touring groups of Australian railway enthusiasts. In fact it was on one of his tours that he first conceived Aus Steam '88 and the plan to run Flying Scotsman as the feature locomotive – a railway royal as guest of honour.

But perhaps it was his experience as Senior Officer of the Diamond Valley group of fire brigades that stood him in best stead during the hectic months of pre-tour organization. 'When you are fighting a bush fire,' he comments, 'you have to keep going, whatever the odds, until you succeed. People just shook their heads when we said that Flying Scotsman was coming, but we forged on and look at the superb results now.'

And forge on Walter did. Highs and lows the whole fascinating operation may have had, but that it succeeded is due so much to Walter Stuchbery's vision.

Walter Stuchbery is Yarrambat's 'postie'.

Opposite: Walter and a Victorian R Class Hudson locomotive.

4472 FLYING SCOTSMAN

No. 4472 Flying Scotsman's visit to Australia in 1988–9 was without question the most exciting railway event in a very long time.

The Gresley Pacific's stately passage through town and country attracted crowds ranging from a few line-side families to thousands of enthusiasts and admirers. From the day in October 1988 when No. 4472 swung ashore from P&O's charter ship *New Zealand Pacific* in Sydney Harbour, people from all over Australia flocked to see this masterpiece from the golden age of British Steam. Then, after trials to comply with the operating requirements of the State Rail Authority of New South Wales, Flying Scotsman set out on an unpublicized run to Melbourne where it was to be the guest of honour at the Bicentennial Steam Celebration. A glimpse of the excitement created by the tour was to be found at a service stop in Goulburn, 225 km (141 miles) south of Sydney. Word-of-mouth ensured that almost 300 avid fans were on hand to welcome No. 4472 and its crew.

Flying Scotsman was the first of Sir Nigel Gresley's Al Pacific engines to be ordered by the newly founded London and North Eastern Railway in 1923. It participated in the British Empire exhibition at Wembley in 1924 and a decade later grabbed headlines for its trial run between London and Leeds when it recorded the first fully authenticated 160 kph (100 mph) run by any steam locomotive.

Flying Scotsman received many modifications over the years. After the nationalization of the railways in Britain in 1948 it received a new road number – 60103 – which it carried until its last journey in revenue service for British Rail in January 1963. Its sisters were sent to the scrap heap, but fortunately not Flying Scotsman. A refit at Doncaster saw it return to the metals for charter and regular tour work, work which often took it to areas not previously visited.

A soundly organized but subsequently ill-fated tour of the United States from 1969 to 1972 almost lost Flying Scotsman for all time. By another stroke of good fortune, however, its present owner, Sir William McAlpine, found No. 4472 and mounted a rescue mission which returned Flying Scotsman to Britain in 1972 and to active duty.

Australians marvelling at Gresley's three-cylinder configuration did not perhaps realize how close that distinctive beat had come to fading away for ever.

4472 and 3801 drift downhill through Clarence in the Blue Mountains of New South Wales.

PARTNERS: 4472 AND 3801

When No. 4472 Flying Scotsman slipped into the platform at Moss Vale in the Southern Highlands of New South Wales on Sunday 18 December 1988 there awaited a truly spectacular scene. On hand to welcome the most famous locomotive in the world was a throng of some 5000 happy people – and two steam-hauled passenger trains.

At the head of one stood D59 Class 2-8-2 No. 5910, splendidly turned out by the New South Wales Rail Transport Museum.

But at the head of the other, standing majestically alongside No. 4472's track, was Australia's best-known and most cherished Pacific locomotive, C38 Class 4-6-2 No. 3801.

It was appropriate that 3801 was there that day formally to welcome Flying Scotsman to New South Wales. The two locomotives had met informally at Aus Steam '88 in Melbourne in October but now the British visitor was on the green streamliner's home ground. Later that same day 4472, heading the train it had hauled from Melbourne, and 3801, leading the Bicentennial carriage set, ran parallel into Sydney's Central Station. It was an emotionally charged moment that no one present will ever forget.

No. 3801, the first of the thirty C38s to be built, was commissioned in 1943. The first five were built by the private firm of Clyde Engineering Co. and were semi-streamlined, featuring the now-famous 'bullet' nose. Nos 3806 to 3830 were built at the railway's own shops at Eveleigh and Cardiff (Newcastle, NSW) and performed equally outstandingly without streamlining. All were in service by 1949.

C38s quickly established themselves as highly efficient performers. Capable of running heavier trains at faster speeds, they could manage up to 450 tons over the rising 1 in 75 gradients of the main southern line to haul the Melbourne Express unassisted over the entire 643 km (402 miles) between Sydney and Albury. So successful was the breed that several units were still in service some fourteen years after dieselization began.

Green-liveried 3801 was rescued from the scrappers in the late 1960s. In 1972 it became the first steam locomotive to cross the Australian continent from Sydney to Perth and in 1985 it was moved to the State Dockyard in Newcastle where it was completely overhauled and rebuilt for its starring role in the Bicentennial celebrations. The parallel run into Sydney that December Sunday was the perfect last rostered duty in one of the busiest years in No. 3801's life.

C38 Class Pacific No. 3807, non-streamlined, *circa* 1949.

Opposite above: 4472 climbs the Cullerin Ranges south of Goulburn on its official entry into New South Wales from Victoria on 18 December 1988.

Opposite below: 3801 climbs to Heathcote Junction in Victoria with the Bicentennial train in 1988.

AFTER A HEAVY SNOWFALL,
NSWGR NN CLASS 3506
BRINGS THE CAVES EXPRESS
INTO MEDLOW BATH,
NEW SOUTH WALES,
CIRCA 1935.

THE NANNY

In November 1923, as No. 4472 was entering service as the Class leader of Sir Niger Gresley's A1 Pacifics, the last of thirty-five 4-6-0 express engines was undergoing trials in far-away New South Wales. The two locomotives had many links, even though they were conceived for duties as far apart as the distance between their manufacture.

Gresley's A1s, later reclassified as A3s, and particularly No. 4472 became famous for their high-speed operations on the LNER British expresses of the day. In contrast, the NN Class of the New South Wales Government Railways was designed by the Chief Mechanical Engineer, Mr E.E. Lucy, who arrived in Australia in 1906 as Assistant CME from the large Wolverhampton shops of the Great Western Railway.

Lucy was promoted to CME in 1911 and immediately set about improving the NSWGR's multi-class fleet of locomotive power. The emphasis at the time was on moving an ever-growing volume of freight, but Lucy turned his mind to the equally pressing need for greater power for the increasingly heavy express passenger services.

Thus was born the NN Class and when the first locomotive rolled out of the Eveleigh (Sydney) workshops in mid-1914 it was compared with Churchill's famous Saint Class which was much of the same vintage. This no doubt was due to Lucy's previous experience. The NN Class was delivered in two batches, however, and later locomotives featured improvements gained from the eight years taken to develop the Gresley Pacifics.

The NNs (or 'Naughty Nannies' as their crews called them) took over mainline services with great enthusiasm. On the fast Sydney–Melbourne expresses they were able to maintain the 96 kph (60 mph) limit with heavier loads while at the same time, through their improved range, they eliminated the need for double-heading and some engine changes.

The Class operated throughout New South Wales until the arrival of the even larger C36 Class 4-6-0 in 1925, after which they spent more time in the north and north-western regions. Plans to rebuild the fleet with all-steel boilers and other new equipment in the early 1950s were shelved when the new generation of diesel-electrics arrived.

The Nannies continued working until 1959, when they began to be withdrawn. Duties in their final years comprised a mixture of local passenger, freight and Hunter Valley coal haulage. The last in service was the Class leader, 3501, which took its final bow on a special outing for enthusiasts in 1968.

Unfortunately the Class was not to work with Flying Scotsman during its tour of New South Wales. Only one Naughty Nannie remains today, a proud exhibit at the New South Wales Rail Transport Museum in Thirlmere.

AUSTRALIAN STEAM

Although in its early days the Australian railway system relied heavily on imported locomotives, principally from Great Britain, in practice the first engines were built in the Colony.

When construction of the Melbourne and Hobson's Bay railway was first mooted nearly 140 years ago, orders were placed with Robert Stephenson & Co. of Newcastle, England, for four 2-4-0 locomotives to be delivered in May 1854. But there were delays in England, and in order that work on the 4.5 km (2.8 mile) track from Melbourne Flinders Street to Port Melbourne – then Sandringham – might continue, the local engineers Robertson, Martin and Smith built a steam locomotive from a 4 hp pile-driving engine and a four-wheel ballast wagon. In July, when it was learned that there were still delays, Robertson, Martin and Smith designed a conventional 2-2-2 locomotive which they built in just eight weeks so that it could enter service in time for the official opening of the first steam railway in Australia on 12 September 1854.

With the age of steam now booming in England, many firms competed for the lucrative business emanating from Australia. And with parochialism supreme among the new colonies, it is little surprise that South Australia's engines came from William Fairbairne of Manchester, Queensland's from Neilson & Co. and Tasmania's from Fox Walker & Co. Robert Stephenson & Co. held the lion's share, however, until Beyer, Peacock & Co. of Manchester entered the market. Admittedly towards the end of the nineteenth century some orders were placed in America, with the Baldwin Locomotive Works featuring strongly. But British influence reigned supreme, not least because the majority of Chief Mechanical Engineers and Locomotive Superintendents of the era were recruited from the major British companies of the day.

This did not deter Australian firms from tendering for and eventually winning orders, of course. Among the more successful enterprises were the Phoenix Foundry of Victoria,

Evans, Anderson & Phelan of Queensland and James Martin of South Australia. And with the approach of the Federation of Australian States in 1901, much greater emphasis was placed on 'home-grown' industry and the railways themselves began to invest in new maintenance workshops to cater for the rapidly expanding network. This was particularly evident at Eveleigh (Sydney), Newport (Melbourne) and Islington (Adelaide).

Although overseas orders for new units were placed right up to the end of the steam era, State railway workshops were soon studying the workings of successful foreign locomotives when new power was under consideration in order to apply the lessons to designs of their own.

In New South Wales, for example, the highly successful C38 Class was designed and developed. The C38s were the Australian-made embodiment of many successful Pacific designs over the previous four decades and had their beginnings back in 1892 with the P6 Class 4-6-0 express engines designed by the NSW railway in conjunction with Beyer Peacock. When these superb locomotives entered service in February 1943, therefore, they embodied fifty years of operating experience in local conditions.

Not until 1951 did another big new passenger locomotive appear on Australian rails. No. 703 was one of seventy mighty R Class 4-6-4 Hudsons to be ordered from the North British Locomotive Works in Glasgow and the first to run on trials later that year.

Nevertheless, it is significant that the last steam locomotive to enter service in Australia involved three of the British firms that had been most associated with steam developments from the very first orders of 1854. For in April 1955 Western Australian Railways took delivery of the first of twenty-four V Class 2-8-2 locomotives for heavy coal haulage in the Collie area. They were designed by Beyer, Peacock & Co. of Manchester and built jointly by Robert Stephenson & Co. and Hawthorns Ltd of Darlington.

Opposite above: 3801 and 3642 – the two largest operative steam locomotives in New South Wales.

Opposite below: A New South Wales Rail Transport Museum special headed by No. 3112 Tank Engine and Nos 3001 and 5910, an American Baldwin imported in 1952.

Opposite above: A Victorian Hudson R Class, No. 766, outside the magnificent Bendigo Locomotive Depot in Victoria.

Opposite below: 3801 and 3813 thunder along at 128 kph (80 mph) south of Bundanoon on a trial run after rebuilding in the early 1970s.

Above left: No. 6029 Beyer Peacock Garratt, lovingly preserved, takes water at Cooma, New South Wales, in the early 1970s.

Above right: The 100-year-old 4-4-0 No. 1210 built by Beyer Peacock approaches Goulburn, New South Wales, on a run from Canberra.

Below left: A South Australian 520 Class built in 1943 climbs through the Adelaide Hills.

Below right: A beautifully restored American Baldwin, No. 5910, waits for the signal at Waterfall, south of Sydney.

A BRIGHT MOONLIT NIGHT AT 3 A.M. –
3611 AND A 38 CLASS WITH THE WESTERN MAIL
BLAST TO THE TOP OF TUMULLA BANK
32 KM (20 MILES) WEST OF BATHURST
IN NEW SOUTH WALES
CIRCA 1960.

THE WESTERN MAIL

In the heyday of steam, Sydney's Central Station was a hive of non-stop activity. Almost all the country departure platforms held rows of passenger carriages together with parcel and mail vans. At the head of each train, with passengers milling to and fro, the elite express locomotives stood aloof, ready to take their loads through the night to far-away destinations in all corners of New South Wales. Even into the 1950s on the Western Line alone five Mails left nightly to climb over the Blue Mountains for Mudgee, Cowra, Forbes, Coonamble and Bourke. The Western Line's great finale was the Through West Mail running between Sydney and Dubbo where passengers changed first into rail cars and later into road coaches for destinations 'further out' in the State.

It was thus entirely fitting that Flying Scotsman's visit to New South Wales should be marked by a re-enactment of the Western Mail's 420 km (262 mile) run. On Friday 9 June 1989 travellers were greeted by the now familiar sight of No. 3801 and No. 4472 Flying Scotsman attached to their train at Central Station in the cool of early evening. Passengers hurried to their seats carrying rugs, supper hampers and modest supplies of liquid refreshment in readiness for the long overnight journey to Dubbo.

Finally all were aboard. Green lights in Sydney Yard signalled the moment of departure and soon the duo were westward bound, streaking towards the horizon as suburban stations flashed by – past Redfern,

past Burwood, past Strathfield and Parramatta and onward until a pause at Penrith at the foot of the Blue Mountains. Locomotives have been drinking and coaling-up here since the 1860s in preparation for the heavy grades (some 1 in 33) so swiftly to come.

Soon the canyons of Lapstone and Glenbrook rumbled to the beat of 4472's triple cylinders and 3801's staccato exhaust. A brief stop at Valley Heights enabled a third locomotive, No. 3112 (a 4-6-4 tank), to be coupled for the steepest section to Katoomba (commemorating the assist engines which performed this duty throughout the steam era).

As the clock ticked into Saturday the train passed over a narrow bridge – the Darling Causeway – at 1100 metres (3350 feet) above sea level, the highest railway point between the Pacific and Indian Oceans. And then began the long downhill run to Lithgow through the ten tunnels opened in 1910 to replace the awesome Great Zig Zag built by John Whitton in the 1860s to get the trains down from the mountains to the Western Plains beyond. From there Flying Scotsman and 3801 sped through the night to Bathurst, Blayney, Orange, Wellington and, with the sun now well down in the sky, to Dubbo.

The rush through the night, the hooting of whistles, the screeching of brakes and the gentle rock of the carriages being pulled at speed and in safety – Flying Scotsman and the green streamliner had done their work and done it well.

Flying Scotsman and No. 3801 thunder west on their re-creation of the Western Mail's run to Dubbo in New South Wales.

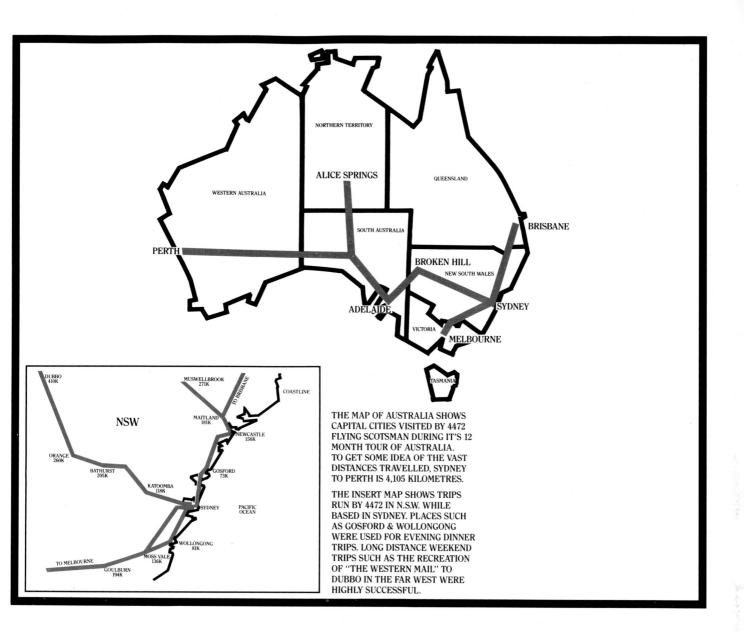

THE MAP OF AUSTRALIA SHOWS CAPITAL CITIES VISITED BY 4472 FLYING SCOTSMAN DURING IT'S 12 MONTH TOUR OF AUSTRALIA. TO GET SOME IDEA OF THE VAST DISTANCES TRAVELLED, SYDNEY TO PERTH IS 4,105 KILOMETRES.

THE INSERT MAP SHOWS TRIPS RUN BY 4472 IN N.S.W. WHILE BASED IN SYDNEY. PLACES SUCH AS GOSFORD & WOLLONGONG WERE USED FOR EVENING DINNER TRIPS. LONG DISTANCE WEEKEND TRIPS SUCH AS THE RECREATION OF "THE WESTERN MAIL" TO DUBBO IN THE FAR WEST WERE HIGHLY SUCCESSFUL.

THE AUSTRALIAN TOUR

On 14 September 1988 No. 4472 Flying Scotsman left Tilbury Docks in London aboard the P&O charter ship *New Zealand Pacific* and arrived in Sydney thirty-two days later. It was unloaded at Wharf 13, Pyrmont, by the floating crane Titan. Thus began an epic journey around Australia of some 44,800 km (28,000 miles).

Flying Scotsman was to haul a striking rake of FS-type and BS-type steel passenger cars built in Sydney by Clyde Engineering Co. in the 1930s. Most were of the compartment type, with beautifully varnished timber and old travelling water-bottles. On some of the longer trips a sleeping car was attached for the crew. Although sitting cars were used on most trips, a notable exception was the Western Mail run in New South Wales which comprised a full set of 1930s' sleepers.

A buffet car was usually attached for morning and afternoon teas and sometimes for à la carte dinners – and, of course, for the famous Australian railway meat pie and frostie. Or for the occasional frozen sandwich at 4 a.m. in the middle of the desert.

No. 4472's runs across Australia were extremely varied and catered for a range of tastes and interests, from a P&O corporate luncheon at a Hunter Valley winery to day trips for the general public to Gosford, Bowral and Wollongong – all within 160 km (100 miles) of Sydney. In Victoria the train could operate only on the Melbourne to Albury run as the rest of the State is one of the few remaining broad-gauge systems in the world. But that was a small price to pay. For wherever Flying Scotsman went in Australia its many hundreds of passengers all enthusiastically agreed on one thing: every trip was an unqualified success.

VICTORIA

From the moment it crossed the Murray River into Victoria, Flying Scotsman attracted enormous attention. Stations were crowded. Traffic on the adjoining Hume Highway slowed and stopped. Every level crossing was a sea of people jostling for vantage-points; farmers and their families perched along every fence in sight. And all to welcome this jewel of British engineering.

At Wangaratta that first day, the crowds were so vast that the train had to slow to walking pace and the north-bound Intercapital Daylight Express was stopped, its tracks blocked by spectators. And so it was all the way to Melbourne, delight turning to open amazement when No. 4472 arrived at the Aus Steam '88 open day at Spencer Street Station where an estimated 130,000 people had come to see Flying Scotsman and a galaxy of visiting locomotives from adjoining States.

In Victoria Flying Scotsman showed its metal by running at speed – and in fine style. The run from Benalla to Seymour, for example, a distance of 100 km (62 miles), was completed start to stop in just 60 minutes. And while the authorized speed was 80 kph (50 mph), 4472 reached a shade under 134 kph (84 mph) on that run.

Running at speed in Flying Scotsman is pure exhilaration. The locomotive is in excellent mechanical condition and under the control of masters of the footplate. Another journey in Victoria took us up to 134 kph (84 mph) before a depletion in coal supply was noticed, but fortunately the line ahead was mostly downhill and good momentum was maintained. The last shovelful of coal hit the fire 25 km (15 miles) out of Melbourne and when 4472 reached Spencer Street the steam gauge was 100 lb below the operating level of 220 lb.

Without doubt, however, it was the parallel runs on the main North Eastern line which provided the greatest excitement. Several times both passengers and line-side spectators were treated to the magnificent sight of Flying Scotsman streaking towards Seymour on the standard-gauge track with two preserved broad-gauge R Class 4-6-4s racing alongside. Even better, and a gesture of farewell as Flying Scotsman swung north for Alice Springs, was the triple parallel run from the northern outskirts of Melbourne to Seymour on 6 August 1989 during Flying Scotsman's second visit to Victoria. No. 4472 occupied the standard gauge, the R Class the Up main and another massive Hudson R Class the Down main. For thousands of happy people, it was a magnificent once-in-a-lifetime sight.

Flying Scotsman's rods await the next call of duty.

Opposite: No. 4472, decked in regalia, waits for the departure signal at Spencer Street Station, Melbourne, at the start of the epic run to Alice Springs.

No. 4472 stands beside a Victorian J Class, one of sixty built in Britain by the Vulcan Foundry, at Seymour in Victoria.

Flying Scotsman, at speed, testing the metals in Victoria.

ON A WARM SPRING DAY,
VICTORIAN S CLASS SIR THOMAS MITCHELL
HEADS AUSTRALIA'S PREMIER TRAIN,
SPIRIT OF PROGRESS, SOUTH OF WANDONG
ON ITS MORNING RUN TO MELBOURNE
CIRCA 1938.

SPIRIT OF PROGRESS

At 6.30 p.m. on Tuesday 23 November 1937, a sleek blue-and-gold passenger train steamed out of Spencer Street Station in Melbourne bound for Albury and Australian railway history.

Named Spirit of Progress, the train was the culmination of a decade of planning by Victorian Railways to provide the ultimate in travel on the crack Melbourne–Albury route, at that time part of the line which linked the capitals of Victoria and New South Wales. The notorious break of gauge at Albury meant that two trains were needed to complete the nightly runs of the Sydney and Melbourne Ltd expresses.

As the Spirit of Progress raced northwards that night it created a most impressive list of 'firsts'. It was the first wholly air-conditioned train, the first all-steel express, the first with a train hostess, the first to run at new high average speeds over the 306 km (191 mile) route and the first in the standards of luxury it offered to all the 400 and more passengers.

The train was the pride of Victorian Railways, having been built in the State's own workshops at Newport. The carriages featured roller-bearing bogies, double-glazed windows, high-tensile steel bodies and deep cushions and carpets throughout. It boasted a dining car and, at the rear, a parlour car from which passengers could see the main North Eastern line unfolding behind.

Power for the mighty express was provided by four S Class Pacific 4-6-2 locomotives first brought into service nearly a decade before. Numbered S-300 to S-303, they were the first three-cylinder express locomotives built in Australia and were now 'dressed' in matching blue-and-gold metal plating around the boiler, cowcatcher and side-sheeting for a semi-streamlining effect. The angled, flat nose with the winged VR crest in gold on the smokebox doors gave them an unmistakable appearance. And they breasted the miles at increasing speeds and with consummate ease: by 1944, S-301, with 528 tons on the draw-gear, covered the 100 km (62 miles) between Benalla and Seymour at an average speed of 115 kph (72 mph).

By 1954 the S Class locomotives had been scrapped in favour of diesel-electrics but the real milestone for the Spirit came in 1962 with the completion of standard-gauge tracks between the State border and Melbourne, thus eliminating the need to change gauge and trains at Albury after a span of more than seventy years.

And so it was that 16 April 1962 found Spirit of Progress standing in Sydney's Central Station ready for the first scheduled direct run through to Melbourne. But the great train took second place that night. Adjacent, on No. 1 platform, stood the newest addition to Australian railways – Southern Aurora, a gleaming fourteen-car sleeper express with the dining and club cars and all the latest appointments.

At Spencer Street in Melbourne the scene was repeated. At exactly eight o'clock that night, the two Southern Auroras left their respective State capitals and raced towards each other, to be followed ten minutes later by the two Spirits of Progress with their sitting cars. It was a scene that was to continue for twenty-five years until the sleeping and sitting trains were amalgamated.

Those keen on railway lore will recall that Spirit of Progress and Southern Aurora, two illustrious names, were replaced with the northbound Sydney Express and the south-bound Melbourne Express – names adopted almost a century before when the rails (albeit of different gauges) first linked Australia's biggest cities.

No. 4472, heading north from Melbourne, near Kilmore in Victoria on the standard gauge. The two tracks in the foreground are broad gauge.

Two Hudson R Class locomotives (*foreground*) line up next to Flying Scotsman and a Vulcan Foundry J Class (*rear*) at Seymour in Victoria on the Alice Springs run.

Overleaf
Dark winter clouds form a backdrop to the spectacular triple parallel run from Melbourne to Seymour during Flying Scotsman's visit to Victoria – Flying Scotsman (*left*) and two R Class locomotives, No. 761 (*centre*) and No. 707 (*right*).

Above left: Footplatemen: Dave Rawlins and Ross Gorman await 4472's departure from Spencer Street Station, Melbourne, on the eve of the run to Alice Springs.

Above right: Flying Scotsman and R Class No. 761 climb up to Glenrowan, Victoria, on the last leg to Albury on the Alice Springs run.

Below: Flying Scotsman arrives in Moss Vale, New South Wales, on 18 December 1988.

Opposite: R Class 761 and No. 4472 running parallel just north of Seymour in Victoria.

NEW SOUTH WALES

As the 'Standard Gauge State', New South Wales was to see more of Flying Scotsman than any other part of Australia. The Gresley Pacific took in its stride the heavy grades of the Blue Mountains, the Hawkesbury River and the South Coast escarpment, and the long level expanse of the inland plains. No. 4472 spent the night in country locomotive depots long dead to the hiss of steam but during the day played to a full house wherever it went.

One trip, out of many, was accomplished against almost overwhelming odds. On Friday 24 March 1989 Flying Scotsman and C38 Class Pacific 3801 steamed out of Sydney's Central Station under cloudy skies and a cool breeze. The two green locomotives were in charge of a twelve-car train and 200 passengers for a run of nearly 1100 km (687 miles) to Brisbane, the capital of the Sunshine State. While regular, air-conditioned sleeping-car expresses cover the journey in some sixteen hours, this tour, with overnight stops at towns en route, was to take four days.

After a canter along the magnificently scenic Hawkesbury River and Central Coast towns, Flying Scotsman and No. 3801 swung inland in light rain for the first overnight stop in Maitland. The next morning, in typically British conditions of fog and increasingly heavy rain, the two locomotives turned off the Great Northern line to attack the mountainous grades and winding route of the North Coast. The rain was by now beating down as the train drove onward through Dungog, Gloucester, Wingham and Taree to the next stopover, Kempsey. As passengers looked through the rain streaking down the carriage windows they could see the surrounding farmland flooding. But even the next day there was still no let up – and nor was there until we met the forbidding McPherson Ranges on the Queensland border.

This is a stretch of rail that never ceases to fascinate the traveller. Climbing all the time, the train winds its way through ravines and glens, passes The Risk (a crossing loop comprising a signal box, some semi-derelict houses, goats and bare-foot children) and approaches the famous Border Loop. Here, the train circumnavigates a mountain by crossing itself twice over, passes through a tunnel and finally emerges in Queensland. And as Flying Scotsman and Pacific No. 3801 raced towards Brisbane on shining ribbons of steel the sun broke through at last to warm the crowds of spectators along the way.

Flying Scotsman and No. 3801 approach the Exeter Bank in the Southern Highlands.

Opposite: No. 4472 (*left*) with the Bicentennial Train and a J Class locomotive at Seymour in Victoria.

Above: On a clear winter morning 4472 and 3801 head north through Mt Colah, a suburb of Sydney.

Below: 4472 and 3801 descend the famous Cowan Bank showing the dense bushlands only 35 km (22 miles) from Sydney.

Rays of evening sunlight pierce the deep cutting of the Cowan Bank as 4472, on a load test, climbs to the top – proving that it could handle 300 tons unassisted.

4472 and 3801 coming through Exeter in the Southern Highlands of New South Wales.

Opposite: Flying Scotsman leaves Goulburn in New South Wales for the last time and heads south to Melbourne.

The return leg of the long run from Sydney to Brisbane and back. After a long haul on the Queensland side of the State border, Flying Scotsman and No. 3801 erupt from the Border Loop tunnel into New South Wales, with passengers frantically ripping open windows to allow fresh air into the stifling cars.

Opposite above: Flying Scotsman and 3801 on the forward journey from Sydney to Brisbane. In pouring rain they climb one of the long grades of the coast of New South Wales near Dungog.

Opposite below: The Brisbane to Sydney run. No. 4472 and 3801 climb to the Border Loop from the Queensland side.

In near freezing conditions on the run to Alice Springs, 4472 blasts out of one of the Bethungra Spiral tunnels in southern New South Wales.

Opposite above: One of the rare occasions that Flying Scotsman was not the lead engine on her Australian tour – NSW 3642 at the head, Bowral, New South Wales.

Opposite below: Flying Scotsman and 3801 roar south across the Bargo viaduct in New South Wales and head for Goulburn.

Overleaf
Left: Flying Scotsman arrives in Hornsby, a suburb of Sydney, to a pipe band welcome and 3000 people.

Right above: On a bright spring morning 4472 waits to depart from Picton, 80 km (50 miles) south of Sydney, on a New South Wales Rail Transport Museum Special.

Right below: On a day trip from Brisbane, 4472 runs into Kyogle on the far north coast of New South Wales.

THE RED HEART

Flying Scotsman's run to the 'Red Heart' – Alice Springs – was not the longest of the visit to Australia (this was to Perth) but it was the most challenging for passengers and spectators alike. Scores of people all over the outback travelled hundreds of miles to see this paragon of steam for themselves. They packed the train on excursions and cheered at every stop.

To the Red Heart began on 6 August 1989 with No. 4472 serviced and ready at Melbourne's Spencer Street Station. On board a select band of passengers was busy stowing clothes, food, books and bottles – it was to be a long trip. Conditions were overcast (Flying Scotsman was getting a name for bringing its own brand of British weather with it).

With a whoosh of triple cylinders 4472 pulled away, bound for Albury and the Murray River for the last time. Beyond lay the main New South Wales southern trunk route to Cootamundra where the train diverted across the New South Wales wheat belt in heavy rain to join the east–west 'Indian Pacific' Sydney–Perth route at Parkes. The run to the Silver City of Broken Hill was just beginning . . .

Opposite: In the Red Heart of a continent: Simpson's Gap, Alice Springs.

Top left: Sunrise in the desert.
Top right: The true red of the outback – rocks in the heat of the day.

Above: 4472 pauses before thundering into the desert.

Opposite: Half the world away from home – Flying Scotsman with the custodians of the outback.

In Alice Springs: Flying Scotsman rests quietly alongside The Ghan, Australia's best-known train.

BEYOND THE BLACK STUMP

Flying Scotsman's run to Broken Hill was one of the most outstanding aspects of the whole tour. To the huge excitement of all concerned, 4472 generated a new world record for a non-stop run by a steam locomotive of 675 km (422 miles)!

From there, Flying Scotsman cantered into South Australia and across the rolling plains to Port Augusta – the real start of the push north into the Red Heart of the continent. As the stark beauty of the Flinders Range faded into the distance, 4472, hampered now by the necessity of pulling a GM diesel, two crew cars and a power car in case of breakdown, for a total of 735 tons, glided inexorably into the land 'beyond the black stump' – land into which even Australian Aborigines rarely venture.

The next stop was Tarcoola – a few scattered houses, a dirt road and a pub. Passengers queued in the freezing night for a seat in its minuscule dining-room and some country hospitality.

Shortly before midnight, No. 4472 rattled over the turnout and became the first steam locomotive to traverse the 'new' standard-gauge line into Alice Springs. Five hours later, the train stopped in what appeared to be the middle of nowhere. Stumbling out of the freezingly cold and antiquated cars, sleepy-eyed passengers stared at a pin-point of light some 5 km (3 miles) away – Marla truckstop, where a pre-dawn breakfast beckoned.

Early that afternoon the long, uncomfortable hours of travel were rewarded. Its triple-cylindered beat thundering over the desert, No. 4472 slipped through the McPherson Gap in the McDonald Ranges and rumbled into Alice Springs.

Opposite above: Flying Scotsman out in the wilderness on the way to Alice Springs. *Opposite below:* 4472 powering through on the run which set a new world record for a non-stop run by a steam locomotive.

THE PERTH MEETING

To reach Western Australia, the last State to be visited on its tour, Flying Scotsman set out to cross a continent. Private sponsors were found, NSW passenger coaches rustled up and Australian national diesels pressed into service to assist No. 4472 across the Nullarbor Plain so that maximum standard-gauge running in Western Australia could be obtained. The trek west began soon after the venture to the Red Heart – Alice Springs.

The journey to the west held another, perhaps emotional theme for Flying Scotsman. On arrival in Perth an old friend was on hand as part of the welcome. For in Britain the Great Western Railway in 1923 produced its own breed of Pacific 4-6-0 locomotives in the 'Castle' Class, and the first produced shared the limelight at the 1924 British Empire exhibition with LNER No. 4472 Flying Scotsman. Another representative, No. 4079 Pendennis Castle, escaped the scrappers in the early 1960s and found a new role in Britain's burgeoning railway movement at Steamtown Railway Museum at Carnforth in Lancashire alongside a certain A3 Pacific . . . 4472 Flying Scotsman.

Then in 1975 a group of Hamersley Iron employees working on the huge mineral railway of the Pilbara region of Western Australia needed a steam locomotive. When none proved available from the standard-gauge state of New South Wales, the members of the Pilbara Railways Historical Society approached Sir Russel Madigan, the Chairman of the Australian Mineral Foundation.

'Don't worry,' he assured the Society's amazed members, 'I'll get you Flying Scotsman.' Not long afterwards came the equally amazing news, 'I couldn't get Flying Scotsman but will Pendennis Castle do?'

Pendennis Castle arrived in its new home on one of the most isolated railways in Australia in April 1978, and when news of Flying Scotsman's proposed visit reached the PRHS, arrangements were made for the two old war-horses of British steam to meet again, this time in Perth and half a world away from home.

It was a wonderful climax to the tour of Western Australia but back in Sydney a ship was waiting. While Pendennis Castle remained in the care of its devoted owners, 4472 returned to New South Wales to be met once again by the premier host, C38 Class Pacific No. 3801. The pair guided the train through the Central West, climbed the Blue Mountains and drifted quietly into Sydney.

In Western Australia – Forrest, a station far out in the featureless wastes of the Nullarbor Plain.

Opposite: Dead level and the longest straight stretch of railway in the world – 478 km (299 miles).

Taking on water: Flying Scotsman and Pendennis Castle.

Opposite above: Pendennis Castle, which performed sterling service in Britain for almost forty years before the Pilbara Railways Historical Society gave it a new home in Western Australia.

Opposite below: 4472 stands quietly after crossing the Australian continent.

FINALE

Flying Scotsman's final journey in Australia was a fitting tribute to the locomotive and to the nation it had conquered.

The plan called for a return trip between Darling Harbour in Central Sydney and Gosford, 90 km (56 miles) up the Main North line on the Central Coast. No. 4472 cantered through the suburbs to Strathfield and swung north on the tight climb to Hornsby, galloped along the Berowra ridge, descended the notorious Cowan Bank to the Hawkesbury River, coursed through the Woy Woy Tunnel and curved around the Brisbane Water shores to Gosford.

After a leisurely lunch while the locomotive was serviced and turned, and with the high tide lapping the pavement way, 4472 set off on the return leg. And from this direction the Cowan Bank presents one of the steepest climbs in the whole Australian railway system. But Flying Scotsman surged effortlessly up the line, clawing at the grade with its triple-cylinder beat echoing from the cliffs above. Scores of fans, aware that this was their last chance to see this magnificent locomotive, lined the trackside to cheer Flying Scotsman on.

The steep climb mastered at last, 4472 breezed back through metropolitan Sydney to Darling Harbour. The final run was completed, the last visitors off the footplate, the platform now silent. After twelve extraordinary months, only the long journey home to Britain remained.

The return leg of the run between Sydney and Gosford was Flying Scotsman's last in Australia – here, 4472 and 3801 climb the Cowan Bank.

Overleaf
Left: Flying Scotsman is prepared at Sydney's No. 13 Wharf, Pyrmont. Its unprotected surfaces are greased against the elements and it is then ready to be lifted offshore by the giant floating crane, Titan.

THE TITAN

In November 1989, Flying Scotsman took leave of Eveleigh Depot and was towed to No. 13 Wharf in Sydney Harbour, Pyrmont. Nearby, waiting, was the Titan, the giant floating crane that is a landmark to match the famous Harbour Bridge. Detached from its tender and secured for travel, No. 4472 was gently affixed to the crane's tackle and hoisted from the wharf. The next morning, the container ship *La Perouse* moved down harbour and slipped into the Pacific Ocean, on its deck a marvel of steam that had captured the hearts of every Australian who saw it – or who had enjoyed the unforgettable pleasure of travelling with Flying Scotsman during the Bicentennial Tour of 1988–9.

Above: High in the air and looking like a toy, 4472 is lifted aboard *La Perouse* in White Bay.

Opposite: La Perouse slips through Sydney Heads on an early November afternoon in 1989, bound for England.